I Am NOT a Penguin

a Penguin

ANIMALS IN THE POLAR REGIONS

BY MARI BOLTE

PEBBLE
a capstone imprint

Published by Pebble, an imprint of Capstone
1710 Roe Crest Drive, North Mankato, Minnesota 56003
capstonepub.com

Library of Congress Cataloging-in-Publication Data
Names: Bolte, Mari, author. Title: I am not a penguin : animals in the Polar regions / Mari Bolte.
Description: North Mankato, Minnesota : Pebble, an imprint of Capstone, [2023]. | Series: What animal am I? | Audience: Ages 5-8. | Audience: Grades K-1. | Summary: "The polar regions are very cold and very windy. There is snow and ice everywhere, but I love my home. My feet help me walk on the slippery ice, but I am not a penguin. My thick fur keeps me warm but I am not an Arctic fox. What animal am I? Read the clues and guess!"—Provided by publisher.
Identifiers: LCCN 2021054284 (print) | LCCN 2021054285 (ebook) | ISBN 9781666343427 (hardcover) | ISBN 9781666343465 (paperback) | ISBN 9781666343502 (pdf) | ISBN 9781666343588 (kindle edition)
Subjects: LCSH: Polar bear—Juvenile literature. | Animals—Polar regions—Juvenile literature. | Polar regions—Juvenile literature. Classification: LCC QL737.C27 B65 2023 (print) | LCC QL737.C27 (ebook) | DDC 599.786—dc23
LC record available at https://lccn.loc.gov/2021054284
LC ebook record available at https://lccn.loc.gov/2021054285

Editorial Credits
Editor: Christianne Jones; Designer: Bobbie Nuytten; Media Researcher: Morgan Walters; Production Specialist: Polly Fisher

Image Credits
Shutterstock: AleksandrN, 20, Middle Right 27, AnnaSmirnova, 16, Top Right 27, Blanka Berankova, (eye) Cover, buchpetzer, 22, Bottom Left 27, chrisontour84, (mountain) Cover, Dotted Yeti, 14, Top Left 27, Fitawoman, 12, Bottom Middle 26, Guoqiang Xue, 8, Middle Left 26, Himanshu Saraf, 28, isabel kendzior, 30Bottom of Form, Jim Cumming, 18, Middle Left 27, JoannaPerchaluk, 10, Middle Right 26, lady-luck, (landscape) design element throughout, Oleksandr Umanskyi, 4, Top Left 26, Scott E Read, 24, Bottom Right 27, Sergey Krasnoshchokov, 6, Top Right 26, yunus topal, spread 2-3

Who Am I?

The polar habitat is home to many kinds of animals. It is where I live. Polar habitats cover the very top and the very bottom of our planet. They are very cold and windy. There is snow and ice everywhere!

But what animal am I? Read the clues to find out!

My wide feet are designed to help me walk on ice and snow. They act like snowshoes. Small bumps on the bottom of my feet keep me from slipping. My toes are also webbed. This helps me swim.

But I am not a penguin.

I migrate when the weather starts to change. Migrating means moving from one area to another.

But I am not a caribou.

My body helps me stay warm in the Arctic cold. I am a hunter. Sometimes I find holes in the ice. There, I wait until I see prey swim by. Then I grab it!

But I am not a snowy owl.

I like to live alone. When it is time to have babies, I dig a den. This keeps them safe.

But I am not an Arctic fox.

My fur is made of two layers. The outer coat is made up of guard hairs. They keep warmth in and water out. My undercoat is thick and warm.

But I am not a musk ox.

I am a mammal. I live in the northernmost part of the Arctic. I hunt mostly in the winter. I dive in the water to hunt fish.

But I am not a narwhal.

I have short ears and a short tail. I can pull them in close to avoid losing body heat. That helps me stay warm even in the coldest weather. My claws help dig in the snow to find food.

But I am not a lemming.

I have large, furry feet. They help me walk on top of the snow. I can reach top speeds of more than 25 miles (40 kilometers) per hour.

But I am not a snowshoe hare.

I like to eat meat. I am not picky about what kind it is. I will eat anything that looks like food. Males of my species are larger than females. I live around 30 years.

But I am not a harp seal.

Hunting seals is the main way I feed myself. Sometimes hunting is hard. If there is not enough food available, I can be a scavenger. That means I eat things that are already dead.

But I am not a killer whale.

I am a huge bear. I weigh as much as 1,700 pounds (771 kilograms). I eat plants and animals. Berries, grass, fruit, birds, and eggs are part of my diet too.

But I am not a grizzly bear.

I am not a penguin

or a caribou

or a snowy owl

or an Arctic fox

or a musk ox

or a narwhal

or a lemming

or a snowshoe hare

or a harp seal

or a killer whale

or a grizzly bear.

So what animal am I?

I am a polar bear!

During the winter, I live on the sea ice. I hunt seals and other ocean prey. In the summer, I live on land. This is because the ice melts. The polar region is the perfect home for me.

COOL FACTS ABOUT
POLAR BEARS

At the beginning of winter, females build dens. Their cubs are born in the middle of winter. Two cubs are most common.

Polar bears are found in the United States, Canada, Russia, Greenland, and Norway.

A polar bear's outer fur is hollow. It reflects light, which is what makes it look white.

Underneath its fur, a polar bear's skin is black. This helps it absorb as much heat as possible.

Although they can run fast for short periods, polar bears do not usually move fast. Their average speed is 3.1 to 3.7 miles (5 to 6 km) per hour.

Books in This Series

Author Bio

Mari Bolte is an author and editor of children's books on all sorts of subjects, from graphic novels about science to art projects to hands-on history. She lives in southern Minnesota in the middle of a forest full of animals.